We Rejoice
in the Light

We Rejoice in the Light

*Candlelighting
Ceremonies
for Advent*

by Sandy Dixon

CBP
CHRISTIAN
BOARD OF
PUBLICATION

St. Louis, Missouri

Cover design: Patrice Holt

Library of Congress Cataloging–in–Publication Data

Dixon, Sandy
  We rejoice in the light: candlelighting ceremonies for Advent / by Sandy Dixon
    p. cm.
    ISBN-13: 978-0-827242-23-4
    ISBN-10: 0-827242-23-9
  1. Advent. 2. Candles and lights. I. Title.
    BV40.D59 1988
    263'.91—dc19   88-7353
                                                                CIP

Printed in the United States of America

Contents

Services for Year C

Year A begins with Advent, 1989, 1992, 1995, etc.

Year B begins with Advent, 1990, 1993, 1996, etc.

Year C begins with Advent, 1988 *, 1991, 1994 *, 1997, etc.

———

* For 1988 and 1994, see Christmas Day (When Christmas Falls on Sunday)

Introduction

Advent is a season of many lights: the Christmas lights decorating town squares, shopping malls, and our own homes. Yet the light we celebrate most at this season is the coming of Jesus.

This collection of Advent candlelighting services is written not simply to consecrate a candle or a symbol, but to help the worshipers relate in a very personal way to the theme of each week, with the hope that the meaning of each week will be something the worshipers will take with them throughout the week and the season.

Although each year's Advent themes are somewhat different and the lectionary readings differ, all are held together, as the title of this resource indicates, by the unifying theme—"We Rejoice in the Light."

These candlelighting ceremonies were originally written for use at Northside Christian Church in St. Louis, using the themes from the sermons of its pastor, the Rev. Marilyn W. Spry. Because they were for a specific church and time, the original text had many local references that were omitted in this publication. Yet it was more meaningful to have these local, personal references. I urge you to find places where you might substitute, for more generic references, ones that can personalize the services for your congregation.

There are many traditions, legends, and customs about the Advent candles, with no clear consensus on what is theologically proper. Usually there are four candles in a circle symbolizing God's endless love. In the center of the circle is a taller candle—the Christ candle—which is lit as part of the Christmas Eve service.

The most common colors for the Advent candles are three purple and one pink, the Christ candle being white. More recently, blue candles are used in the Advent wreath. But it is just as acceptable to use all white, all purple, or all blue candles. The colors of the Advent candles carry the symbolism of the season. The white of the Christ candle reminds us of the purity of Christ. If blue candles are used, they represent love and hope. The purple candles stand for royalty. If a pink candle is used with three purple, it is lit on the fourth Sunday. Tradition says that this is the "rose" candle, signifying the perfectness of the flower of Christ. This captures the symbolism of the Advent hymn, "Lo, How a Rose E'er Blooming."

With all the legends and traditions to guide us, it is still up to us how we celebrate and participate in Advent. The symbolism—or rather the actuality of the light in our midst—becomes more meaningful as we see the candles lit, brightening not only the sanctuary, but also the darkening December days. As each candle is lit, as the sanctuary becomes brighter, as the scriptures are read—full of promise and hope—the light of Christ is freshly lit within us.

Instructions for Use

These Advent candlelighting services are for use on Sunday mornings during the first part of the worship service. From one to three people may be used: an acolyte, a leader, and (if desired) a reader for the meditation.

During the opening hymn, the acolyte (with candlelighter lit) and the leader(s) will process to the chancel. The acolyte will stand beside the Advent wreath, and the leader(s) will move to appropriate places for public reading (lectern, pulpit, microphone). The leader will ask people to join in the Litany of Light, while the congregation remains standing. When the litany is finished, the congregation will be seated.

The candle for each preceding Sunday is relit as the leader names them. The leader (or reader) then reads the meditation for the day, and the acolyte lights the candle for the week. Then the leader leads the congregation in the collect, or unison prayer. At the conclusion, the acolyte and leader(s) may exit as the organist plays through a reprise of the opening hymn.

In addition to the services for the four Sundays of Advent, a special service for the Sunday after Christmas is provided. Our Advent and Christmas decorations in the sanctuary often disappear into the closets and storage rooms without a sense of closure or transition from this celebrative season. This service provides a conclusion for the Advent/Christmas season. Although each year's services are handled a bit differently, in each, the four Advent candles are put out in an extinguishing ceremony. The Christ candle remains lit, witnessing to the light of Christ in our lives throughout the year. The candlelighting taper is relit from the Christ candle, and the Christ candle is extinguished. The acolyte proceeds out, carrying forth the light as a witness and example of our carrying our light into the world.

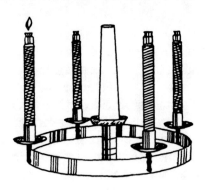

Year A

First Sunday of Advent
Scriptures:
Psalm 122
Isaiah 2:1-5
Romans 13:11-14
Matthew 24:36-44

Theme: Expectation

Litany of Light*

LEADER: Let us share together in the Litany of Light.

LEADER: I rejoiced when they said to me:

PEOPLE: Let us go to the house of the Lord!

LEADER: Pray for peace in Jerusalem.

PEOPLE: Pray for peace inside your city walls.

UNISON: Since all are my neighbors and friends I say, Peace be with you.

LEADER: Since Yahweh our God lives here, I pray for your good.

---

*Litanies of Light in Year A are adapted from *Psalms Anew*, by Nancy Schreck, OSF, and Maureen Leach, OSF (St. Mary's Press, 1986). Used by permission.

Meditation

We are expecting,
waiting, anticipating,
like a couple expecting
their first child.
We, too, are expecting a Child.
It's not a new birth.
We've observed it before,
and we'll observe it again.
But it's the birth of a Child
who will change our lives.
As the couple expecting their
first child,
we are uncertain
what change that
Child will bring.
So, even though
we're expecting, . . .
there is still the unexpected,
the unknown.
But we have an advantage,
"inside information."
Because we are believers in

a Loving God,
And followers of a Living Christ,
we know more what to expect.
This Christmas, we know
that the
expectation, the waiting,
the anticipation
can mean
better things,
a new life,
new chances—
all because of an
expected, and an
unexpected, birth.

LEADER: Today we light the first candle of Advent—the Light of Expectation.

Lighting of the First Advent Candle

Collect (Unison)

O Giver of life, give us patience and hope as we wait for the coming of a Child—the Christ—who has the power to change and renew us continually. Amen.

(At the close of the prayer, the organist will play softly a verse of the opening hymn as the acolyte and Advent leader leave the chancel.)

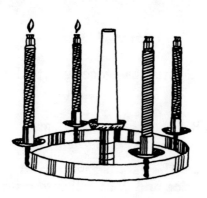

Second Sunday of Advent
Year A   *Scriptures:*
        Psalm 72:1-8
        Isaiah 11:1-10
        Romans 15:4-13
        Matthew 3:1-12

Theme: Preparation

Litany of Light*

LEADER: Let us share together in the Litany of Light.

LEADER: O God, with your judgment and with your justice, endow the leaders.

PEOPLE: They shall govern your people with justice and your afflicted ones with righteousness.

LEADER: Blessed be their name forever; their name shall remain as long as the sun.

PEOPLE: In them shall all the nations of the earth be blessed; all the nations shall proclaim their happiness.

LEADER: Blessed be Yahweh, the God of Israel, who alone does wondrous deeds.

UNISON: And blessed forever be God's glorious name; may the whole earth be filled with God's glory.

(At the close of the litany, ask the people to

be seated, then say—)

LEADER: Last week we lit the candle of Expectation.

Lighting of the Previous Advent Candle

Meditation

We have expected the
baby Jesus,
the Christ.
But no arrival is complete
without the preparation.
We are "getting our act together"
or "ourselves in gear"
as the popular expressions go.
But preparation is somewhat
different from expectation.
Expectation, waiting, can be
passive, non-active.
But preparation needs ACTION

on our part.
Whatever we prepare for,
we're busy doing—
like preparing for
Christmas for instance.
We cook
bake
buy
eat
wrap
give
receive
decorate.
All of these are active—
we have participated.
This Christmas we must
most of all prepare
for Christ.
In our lives, we must actively
make straight the way of the Lord,
to help with justice
and righteousness,
and we will know that we
have prepared well

when we feel the blessing of Christ.

LEADER: We will now light our new candle of Preparation.

Lighting of the Second Advent Candle

Collect (Unison)

Prepare our hearts, O God, to receive you this Advent; but even more, prepare our hearts to be open to your way of justice and righteousness and prepare our lives to reflect your way. Amen.

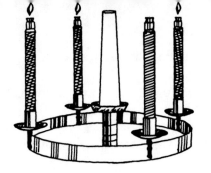

Third Sunday of Advent
Year A *Scriptures:*
Psalm 146:5-10
Isaiah 35:1-10
James 5:7-10
Matthew 11:2-11

Theme: Purpose

Litany of Light

LEADER: Let us share together in the Litany of Light.

LEADER: Happy are those whose help is the God of Jacob and Rachel, whose hope is in Yahweh their God.

PEOPLE: Yahweh, you set captives free.

MEN: And give sight to the blind.

WOMEN: You raise up those that were bowed down.

UNISON: And love the just.

LEADER: You protect strangers;

WOMEN: The orphan and widow you sustain.

MEN: But the way of the wicked you thwart.

UNISON: Yahweh shall reign forever your God, O Zion, through all generations.

LEADER: We have previously lit the candles of Expectation and Preparation. Later today we will be lighting the candle of Purpose.

Lighting of the Previous Advent Candles

Meditation

We have spent long weeks
it seems,
expecting and
preparing.
The anticipation and hard
work of preparing
have heightened the
Christmas spirit in us—
yet,
but,
How many times
have you wondered,
"Why do I do all this?
Each year I do more and more.
I'm so tired of all this.

Why must Christmas be so frantic?"
The psalmist said words about God
setting captives free,
giving sight to the blind,
protecting strangers,
and helping widows and orphans.
In the scripture you will hear
Jesus telling about
the healings
and the opportunities.
It's easy to say "That's nice,"
and wonder just how the
expectation, the anticipation,
and the preparation
can be related
to all the good things we've heard.
The prophet Jeremiah
told his people that God
had plans for them—
a future and a hope.
We know from many Christmases
followed by many Easters
that birth is followed
by life,

followed by death—
but that death is followed
by life.
We are aware of God working
in our lives
for good,
for healing,
for salvation,
for possibilities,
and as one biblical scholar
puts it,
for amazement!
That is the why,
the connection,
the purpose,
the reason.
And if any person or event
is worth expecting
or preparing for,
Jesus, our Savior, is!

LEADER: Today we light the candle of
Purpose

Lighting of the Third Advent Candle

Collect (Unison)

Our Creator and Savior, thank you for having plans for us your people. During this celebrative season help us to realize that your plans are for good, and that we are, indeed, recipients of this wonderful plan. Amen.

Fourth Sunday of Advent
Year A   *Scriptures:*
                    Psalm 24
                    Isaiah 7:10-16
                    Romans 1:1-7
                    Matthew 1:18-25

Theme: Presence

Litany of Light

LEADER: Let us share together in the Litany of Light.

LEADER: The world and all that is in it belong to Yahweh; the earth and all who live in it.

PEOPLE: Yahweh built it on the deep waters, laid its foundations in the ocean's depths.

LEADER: Who has the right to climb Yahweh's mountain? Or stand in this holy place?

MEN: Those who are pure in act and thought.

WOMEN: Who do not worship idols or make false promises.

LEADER: Yahweh will bless them. God their Savior will give them salvation.

(After the people are seated, the Advent leader speaks.)

29

LEADER: In past weeks we have lit candles of Expectation, Preparation, and Purpose. Today we celebrate experiencing Christ's *Presence.*

Lighting of the Previous Advent Candles

Meditation

What is Jesus' name?
Christ, . . .
Lord, . . .
Savior . . . .
Isaiah says his name
will be called
Wonderful Counselor
Mighty God,
Everlasting Father,
Prince of Peace.
What majestic images!
What glorious music we
hear in our minds as we
replay

the carols,
the cantatas,
the oratorios
with these words.
But Matthew, quoting Isaiah,
says his name shall be called
Emmanuel, which means God with us.
GOD WITH US!
God with us.
God with us continually,
personally,
forever,
always . . . .
God's presence
filling us,
guiding us,
comforting us,
encouraging us.
God with us
challenging us
to new possibilities,
giving us courage to go on.
God with us
giving us

31

his Son,
our Savior,
who *is*
Emmanuel.
God with us!

LEADER: Let us light the candle of Presence.

Lighting of the Fourth Advent Candle

Collect (Unison)

God of us all, we thank you for giving us your Son as a very personal Savior. We know he is always with us, and we rejoice in his presence. Amen.

The Sunday After Christmas
Year A   *Scripture:*
                  Psalm 111

Lighting of the Candles

Litany of Light

LEADER: Let us share together in the Litany of Light.

PEOPLE: Alleluia! I will thank you, Yahweh, with all my heart, in the meeting of

the just and their assembly.

WOMEN: Great are your works to be pondered by all who love them.

MEN: Glorious and sublime are your works; your justice stands firm forever.

LEADER: You help us remember your wonders. You are compassion and love.

WOMEN: You give food to those who fear you; keeping your covenant ever in mind.

UNISON: You have shown your might to your people by giving them the lands of the nations.

LEADER: Your works are justice and truth; your precepts are all of them sure.

MEN: They are steadfast forever and ever—made in uprightness and faithfulness.

LEADER: You have sent deliverance to your people and established your covenant forever. To fear you is the beginning of wisdom; all who do so prove themselves wise.

UNISON: Your praise shall last forever!

(The Litany of Light will be followed by the "Gloria Patri.")

Meditation

During December which is the
month of Advent,
we have observed a
paradox . . . .
December has the
shortest days of the year.
Our days are darker.
But in our worship service,
we have begun to
draw our attention to the
Light.
Our sanctuary is
increasingly brightened
as each Sunday
another candle is lit
in our Advent wreath.

We hear scriptures
that speak of light . . .
"The people who walked
in darkness have seen
a great light."
"In him was life and the
light of men. The light shines
in the darkness and the
darkness has not overcome it."
We have become used to the idea of
light overcoming darkness.
The symbolic hope and light
have become
our *real* hope and light,
as we have once again
participated in the
birth of Christ.
Yet today, even with
all the Advent candles
and especially the Christ
candle lit,
we are aware of the
ending of the Christmas celebration.
Today at the end of our service,

the candles will be
extinguished.
It is winter.
It is dark.
Advent and Christmas are over.
But wait.
Listen, "The light shines
in the darkness and the
darkness has not overcome it."
Look, the flame from the
Christ candle,
the Light of the world,
will go forth,
leading us out
into the world,
to give us hope renewed
as we remember
that, even though
it is winter,
Now the days are a
bit longer.
Now there is more light.
And we have
light and hope

in our lives from
once more
participating and
experiencing
the Light of Jesus Christ
in this Christmas season.

Collect (Unison)

We are grateful, O Giver of Light, for your
gift to us of your light—Jesus Christ. Enable us
to keep that light of hope and life burning in us
as we live the Christian life. Amen.

*(At the end of the worship service, the aco-
lyte will go to the Advent wreath and begin
to extinguish the four Advent lights. Then,
take the light from the Christ candle with the
taper, extinguish the Christ candle, and
stand at the wreath while the congregation
says the response.)*

LEADER: Thank you God for the Light that has lightened our place of worship.

PEOPLE: Thank you for the Light which has been sent into our lives.

UNISON: Let us follow the Light into the world; enable us to be bearers of that Light, which your son Jesus Christ has shown us. Amen.

Carrying Forth the Light

(The choir may sing "I Want to Be a Child of the Light"** or an appropriate closing hymn. As they sing, the acolyte, with lit candlelighter, leaves the sanctuary followed by the minister.)

———

** by Kathleen Thomerson © 1970—the Fishermen, Inc. (Redeemer Books, 4411 Dallas, Houston, TX 77023).

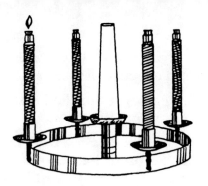

Year B

First Sunday of Advent
Scriptures:
Psalm 80:1-7
Isaiah 63:16—64:8
1 Corinthians 1:3-9
Mark 13:32-37

Theme: Watch

Litany of Light

LEADER: Let us share together in the Litany of Light.

LEADER: From of old no one has heard or perceived by the ear;

PEOPLE: No eye has seen a God besides thee—

LEADER: Who works for those who watch for him—

UNISON: Let us not lack in any spiritual gifts as we wait for the revealing of our Lord Jesus Christ.

Meditation

Today our Advent theme is Watch. This is the first Sunday of Advent. In some churches, the season from Pentecost to Advent is called "ordinary time"—about six months of the usual, ordinary, day-to-day part of the church

41

year. But today we begin the celebration of Advent.

Watch.

Remember the old marquee heading, "Watch this space for coming attractions"? Isn't that a way we can understand Advent? Soon we will be decorating the sanctuary, and we'll celebrate that. Each week in Advent, help us watch this space—this space in our church, this space in our hearts and minds. We *watch* for *the Advent*, the beginning of a new church year and its first festival, Christmas.

LEADER: Today we light the candle that reminds us to Watch.

Lighting of the First Advent Candle

Collect

God, as we do each Advent season, again this year we pray that you will help us watch for your coming and your being active in our lives. Amen.

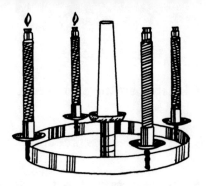

Second Sunday of Advent
Year B   *Scriptures:*
          Psalm 85:8-13
          Isaiah 40:1-11
          2 Peter 3:8-15a
          Mark 1:1-8

Theme: Prepare

Litany of Light

LEADER: Let us share together in the Litany of Light.

LEADER: In the wilderness prepare the way of the Lord.

PEOPLE: Make straight in the desert a highway for our God.

LEADER: Every valley shall be lifted up, and every mountain and hill shall be made low.

PEOPLE: The uneven ground shall become level and the rough places a plain.

UNISON: And the glory of the Lord shall be revealed.

LEADER: Last week we lit the candle calling us to Watch. Today our theme is Prepare.

Lighting of the Previous Advent Candle

Meditation

"Prepare ye the way of the Lord," speaks John the Baptist, echoing Isaiah, crying in the wilderness. Have you heard the song by that name from the gospel musical *Godspell*? It begins slowly, deliberately, in a processional rhythm. Gradually it builds in loudness, beat, tempo, and joy, until as you listen, you begin clapping, tapping your foot, and maybe even moving your body to the rhythm.

Prepare.

Isn't that the way our preparations usually run during the course of the Advent season? After Thanksgiving we begin slowly to think about what needs doing, and we begin deliberately doing each thing. Within days, though, it seems we are frantically trying to get everything done. Perhaps in this accelerating pace, we need to stop and deliberately think of how we "prepare the way of the Lord." Our best preparation might be found in quiet meditation, Christian service, or by giving of ourselves and sharing the joyfulness of the Christmas season.

LEADER: Today we light the candle of Preparation.

Lighting of the Second Advent Candle

Collect

God, we have been watching for your presence. Help us now to prepare the way for you to come into our lives and hearts. Amen.

Third Sunday of Advent
Year B *Scriptures*:
Isaiah 61:1-4, 8-11
Luke 1:46b-55
1 Thessalonians 5:16-24
John 1:6-8, 19-28

Theme: Build

Litany of Light

LEADER: Let us share together in the Litany of Light.

LEADER: The Spirit of the Lord God is upon me because the Lord has anointed me to bring good tidings to the afflicted.

PEOPLE: God has sent me to bind up the brokenhearted;

MEN: To proclaim liberty to the captives;

WOMEN: And the opening of the prison to those who are bound;

LEADER: And to proclaim the year of the Lord's favor.

UNISON: The Lord God will cause righteousness and praise to spring forth before all the nations.

LEADER: On the preceding Sundays we have lit candles reminding us to watch and prepare. This Sunday the theme is Build.

48

Meditation

Close your eyes and think of building. What images come to mind? Do you envision a large skyscraper under construction? Do you see the large boom crane rising from the middle of the building under construction, hanging out over the streets? Do you think of children playing and building structures out of wood blocks?

Now open your eyes and look around the sanctuary. What do you see being built that is connected with Advent? Each week, as our sanctuary has been decorated and as we have added to the light of our Advent candles, we have been building.

As we celebrate Advent, or any time of the year, we can build our Christian lives by putting our faith into action. The largest building begins with a foundation, and goes up from there. So it is with the kingdom of God.

LEADER: Let us light the candle that reminds us to Build.

Lighting of the Third Advent Candle

Collect (Unison)

God, we have been watching for your coming and preparing for your arrival. Help us build in our lives a structure worthy of your coming. Amen.

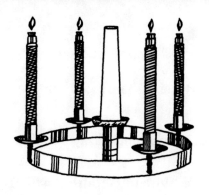

Fourth Sunday of Advent
Year B   *Scriptures*:
Psalm 89:1-4, 19-24
2 Samuel 7:8-16
Romans 16:25-27
Luke 1:26-38

Theme: Glory

Litany of Light

LEADER: Let us share together in the Litany of Light.

LEADER: I will sing of thy steadfast love, O Lord, forever.

PEOPLE: With my mouth, I will proclaim thy faithfulness to all generations.

LEADER: For thy steadfast love was established forever, and thy faithfulness is firm as the heavens.

PEOPLE: Thou hast said, "I have made a covenant with my chosen one ...

UNISON: I will establish your descendants forever, and build your throne for all generations."

LEADER: We have been called in other weeks to Watch, to Prepare, to Build, and have lit candles reminding us of those words. Today we begin to receive God's Glory.

Lighting of the Previous Advent Candles

Meditation

When else but in the Christmas season do we often use the word *Glory?* How many carols and anthems of Christmas use the word?

Glory to God in the Highest!

Gloria, Gloria, Gloria, in Excelsis Deo!

Glory to the newborn King!

Glory. Praise. Honor. Splendor. Exaltation. All are words used to describe the presence of God and God's wonderful act of reaching out to us in a human way through Jesus. We have accepted this reaching out, or we wouldn't be here today. But it doesn't end here. Our response is in each moment of our lives. With each prayer, with each act of Christian love, in every day of our lives, God is praised. Glory be to God!

LEADER: Let us light the candle of Glory.

Lighting of the Fourth Advent Candle

Collect (Unison)

God, in longing we have watched. In eagerness we have prepared. We have been carefully building. Now we see your glory and give you glory! Amen!

The Sunday After Christmas
Year B   *Scriptures*:
           Isaiah 61:10—62:3

Theme: Light

Lighting of the Candles

Litany of Light

LEADER: Let us share together in the Litany of Light.

LEADER: The people who walked in darkness have seen a great light.

PEOPLE: Those who dwelt in a land of deep darkness, on them has light shined.

LEADER: The light shines in the darkness and the darkness has not overcome it.

UNISON: For to us a child is born, a Son is given. In him was life and the life was the light of all peoples.

LEADER: Over the past month, we have watched, and in preparation we have been building in order to be in readiness to receive God's glory. Now we live in the *light* of God's glory.

Meditation

Today is the first Sunday all the candles of our Advent wreath have been lit. On Christmas Eve we lit the Christ candle. And now the circle of light with the center of Christ is complete.

Do you remember the awe of that moment in our Christmas Eve service when all the candles were lit? The sanctuary had gone from near darkness to a glow of light.

The Gospel of John describes Christ as a candle. Jesus was born in a dark day not unlike the ones we live in. But a light has been lit; and it remains lit. And by that light Christ is revealed in hope, goodness, Christian love, Christian service, prayers asked, and prayers answered.

It may seem that the watching, the preparing, the building, and perhaps even the glory of Christmas have diminished a bit. The decorations are getting a bit bedraggled; the tree looks forlorn without packages; and the anticipation and excitement are over.

But the most important part of the festive holiday remains each year and always—the revelation, the incarnation, the birth of Jesus Christ who gives light to each of us.

Collect (Unison)

God, let us not think that the watching, preparing, and building are over, that the glory is past. Help us to live continually in the light of the living Christ. Amen.

(At the end of the worship service, the acolyte will go to the Advent wreath and begin to extinguish the four Advent lights. Then, the acolyte will take the light from the Christ candle with the taper, extinguish the Christ candle, and stand at the wreath while the congregation prays in unison.)

Prayer (Unison)

This one light remains in our hearts, reminding us that the Word has become flesh and dwells among us. Let Christ's love shine in the darkest corner of our lives. Let Christ's love shine in the darkest corners of our world. God is with us. Alleluia.*

Carrying Forth the Light

(The choir may sing "When the Earth Shall Be Filled with Glory"** or an appropriate closing hymn. As they sing, the acolyte, with candlelighter lit, leaves the sanctuary followed by the minister.)

---

* Adapted from a benediction by Ruth C. Duck, *Bread for the Journey*, (Pilgrim Press, 1981), p. 26.

** Words by A.C. Ainger, music by Austin Lovelace. Copyright 1980, Art Masters Studios, Inc. (2614 Nicollet Ave., Minneapolis, MN 55408).

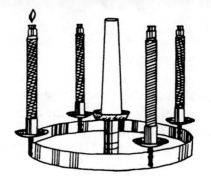

Year C

First Sunday of Advent
Scriptures:
Psalm 25:1-10
Jeremiah 33:14-16
1 Thessalonians 3:9-13
Luke 21:25-36

Theme: Hope

Litany of Light

LEADER: Let us share together in the Litany of Light.

LEADER: To thee, O Lord, I lift up my soul.

MEN: O my God, in thee I trust.

WOMEN: Make me to know thy way, O Lord.

UNISON: Teach me thy paths.

MEN: Lead me in thy truth and teach me.

WOMEN: For thou art the God of my salvation.

UNISON: For thee I wait all the day long.

Meditation

How many times this fall did you hear, "I sure hope my favorite team wins the World Series"? When you were a child, did you ever say, "I sure hope I get the doll with the blond hair—or the shiny red bicycle—for Christmas"? It's a fact that our team doesn't always win the big game, and we probably didn't get everything we wanted each Christmas.

For generations the Jews had waited and hoped for a messiah—a redeemer, a savior. Their hope wasn't a shallow, empty hope for material possessions or a title, but a hope that God would enter their lives. The Jewish people trusted and waited for God to act. They never gave up hope. Learning and doing God's way was part of their waiting for the Savior, as waiting is a real part of our hope.

LEADER: Let us light the candle of Hope, the first of our Advent candles.

Lighting of the First Advent Candle

Collect (Unison)

God, like the Jews of long ago, we wait for you to enter our lives. We know indeed that you have entered through the sending of Jesus.

While we wait this Advent season, let us constantly see our hope fulfilled as we see your love at work in our lives. Amen.

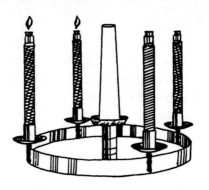

Second Sunday of Advent
Year C   *Scriptures:*
                    Psalm 126
                    Malachi 3:1-4
                    Philippians 1:3-11
                    Luke 3:1-6

Theme: Salvation

Litany of Light

LEADER: Let us share together in the Litany of Light.

LEADER: When the Lord restored the fortunes of Zion, we were like a dream.

UNISON: Then our mouths were filled with laughter and our tongues with shouts of joy.

MEN: They said among the nations: The Lord has done great things for them.

WOMEN: The Lord has done great things for us.

UNISON: We are glad!

LEADER: Last week we lit the candle of Hope (*acolyte will relight the first candle*). Today our theme is Salvation.

Lighting of the Previous Advent Candle

Meditation

"Count your blessings, name them one by one . . . and it will surprise you what the Lord has done." I imagine most of you remember that gospel hymn. Have you ever tried to make a list of your blessings—home, food, friends, family, freedom to worship? We could go on and on.

The Psalm that we just read responsively refers to the people returning from many years in exile in another country. Their blessing was the return to their homeland. They enthusiastically praised God for acting in their lives. Perhaps the biggest blessing, which we often take for granted, is Jesus, our salvation. More often than just during Advent and Christmas we need to remember that God has done great things for us, and that we *are* glad.

LEADER: We will now light the candle of Salvation.

Lighting of the Second Advent Candle

Collect (Unison)

We, like the Jews of old, are grateful for your works, O God. Remind us again, during this Advent, and keep us mindful during the whole year, that the greatest thing you did for us was the giving of your son Jesus—our salvation. Amen.

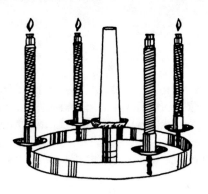

Third Sunday of Advent
Year C   *Scriptures:*
Psalm 97
Zephaniah 3:14-20
Isaiah 12:2-6
Philippians 4:4-9
Luke 3:7-18

Theme: Renewal

Litany of Light

LEADER: Let us share together in the Litany of Light.

LEADER: The Lord reigns.

PEOPLE: Let the earth rejoice.

WOMEN: The heavens proclaim his righteousness.

MEN: All the people behold his glory.

LEADER: Light dawns for the righteous and joy for the upright in heart.

UNISON: Rejoice in the Lord, O you righteous, and give thanks to his holy name.

LEADER: On other Sundays, we have lit candles signifying Hope and Salvation. Today we will be thinking about Renewal.

Lighting of the Previous Advent Candles

Meditation

All of us have received renewal notices for our magazine subscriptions, and have been called to "renewal" in that way. In September, many Christians emphasize church loyalty and the renewal of commitment to the church. Sometimes couples will celebrate a wedding anniversary by renewing their marriage vows. The psalmist uses the image of dawn as renewal. "Light dawns for the righteous." The dawn of each new day is a sign of renewal—a new beginning. God never fails to give us a new dawn, a renewal, new opportunities—and it is a reality in the sending of Jesus, whose birth we are anticipating.

LEADER: Today we will light the third candle—that of Renewal.

Lighting of the Third Advent Candle

Collect (Unison)

O Giver of Light, especially this Advent season, let us remember that each new dawn gives us renewal, opportunities not only to affirm our commitment to you and to serve you but to rejoice and give thanks to you. Amen.

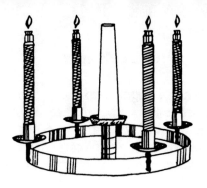

Fourth Sunday of Advent
Year C   *Scriptures:*
                    Psalm 98
                    Micah 5:2-5
                    Hebrews 10:5-10
                    Luke 1:39-55

Theme: Joy

Litany of Light

LEADER: Let us share together in the Litany of Light.

LEADER: Make a joyful noise to the Lord: all the earth.

WOMEN: Break forth into joyous song!

MEN: Sing praises!

LEADER: Sing praises to the Lord with the lyre.

WOMEN: With the lyre and the sound of a melody.

MEN: With trumpets and the sound of a horn.

UNISON: Make a joyful noise before the King, the Lord.

LEADER: We have seen the candles of Hope, Salvation, and Renewal lit. Today our theme is Joy.

Lighting of the Previous Advent Candles

Meditation

Is there any way at all that we cannot say this Psalm joyfully? In fact, you may want to sing it. Maybe you have heard an anthem joyfully using these words. Or think of songs that have the word "happy" in them. Did you think of these: "Happy Days Are Here Again," "If You're Happy and You Know It, Clap Your Hands," "I Want to Be Happy," and from the *Peanuts* musical, "Happiness Is Two Kinds of Ice Cream." Compare these fun words with the great *joy* and *depth* of the Psalm—or with the angels announcing the birth of Jesus. They didn't proclaim a mere happiness: They proclaimed a great JOY!

We need to be a people of great joy, making a joyful noise! It is good to have Advent to remind us. Our themes for the last three weeks have been hope, salvation, and renewal. We have *hope*; and our hope is fulfilled in Jesus, our *salvation*. We always have a chance for *renewal*. Hope, salvation, and renewal are certainly worth being *joyous* about.

LEADER: This morning we will light the fourth candle; that of Joy.

Lighting of the Fourth Advent Candle

Collect (Unison)

We pray in thanksgiving to you, O Giver of great joy, for the gifts of hope, salvation, and renewal. Keep that joy growing in us. Amen.

The Sunday After Christmas
Year C   *Scriptures:*
                       Psalm 111

Lighting of the Candles

(Acolyte lights all candles during the pre-lude, this Sunday only.)

Litany of Light

LEADER: Let us share together in the Litany of Light.

LEADER: Praise the Lord!

UNISON: I will give thanks to the Lord with my whole heart.

LEADER: Great are the works of the Lord.

UNISON: He has caused his wonderful works to be remembered.

LEADER: He has shown his people the power of his works,

UNISON: In giving them the heritage of the nations.

Meditation

This is the week when our Christmas decorations at home begin to look forlorn and droopy. The tree, a few weeks ago green and fragrant, now is dull and dry. Without the gifts to brighten the floor underneath it, the tree has lost its excitement. The decorations, which added color and brightness, are now beginning to look as though they now add clutter. We often get anxious to get it all packed up, put away, carried to the attic, the basement, or the closet, so we can vacuum the whole house thoroughly for the first time since we decorated for Christmas. We breathe a sigh of relief. Christmas is over for another year.

And look at the sanctuary. This is the fifth Sunday since Advent started, and we have gone through the candlelighting ceremonies. We've seen the sanctuary greens and the nativity set for many weeks now. Probably sometime during the week ahead, the worship committee or janitor will take these decorations down and put them away until next Advent.

At home, in the towns, at work, at church, everything will be back to normal again.

But are our lives really back to normal? Is everything the same?

78

Think and reflect upon what we have heard this Advent and Christmas—the hope of a savior coming, our salvation, the renewal of our lives in the coming of Jesus. The joy of knowing Jesus our Savior—our lives have been touched and changed by these words.

We *will* remember the light that these words have given for us. As we have celebrated Christmas, once again we have been not only *reminded* but we have *experienced* God's great love for us. And that light will remain with us.

Collect (Unison)

We know you are always constant in your love and mercy for us, God. Yet we also realize you are always giving us new ways to experience you. We thank you that once again we are touched and changed by the celebration of the birth of Jesus Christ. Help us to be witnesses to that renewal in us. Amen.

(At the end of the worship service, the aco-

lyte will extinguish all but the Christ candle, relight the candlelighter, and then extinguish the Christ candle.)

MINISTER: God has sent redemption to his people.

UNISON: He has commanded his covenant forever.

MINISTER: Holy is his name.

UNISON: His praise endures forever.

Carrying Forth the Light

(The readers and acolyte will proceed with the lit candlelighter out of the sanctuary.)

Benediction

Go forth enabled with the light of God's love. Carry it joyously in your life, knowing that you are redeemed and forgiven by Christ. We walk in the light of God's grace. Amen.

Choral Response

(The choir may sing "I Want to Be a Child of the Light,"* or an appropriate closing hymn. As the choir sings, the acolyte, with lit candlelighter, leaves the sanctuary followed by the minister.)

-----

* by Kathleen Thomerson © 1970—the Fishermen, Inc. (Redeemer Books, 4411 Dallas, Houston, TX 77023).

Christmas Day (Sunday)
Scriptures:
Luke 2:1-12
Titus 2:11-14
Psalm 96
Isaiah 9:2-7

Lighting of the Candles

The Litany of Light

LEADER: Let us share together in the Litany of Light.

LEADER: O sing to God a new song: Sing to God all the earth.

PEOPLE: Sing to God, bless his name; tell of his salvation from day to day.

LEADER: The people who walked in darkness have seen a great light.

PEOPLE: Those who dwelt in the land of darkness, on them has light shined.

LEADER: For to you is born this day a Savior who is Christ the Lord!

PEOPLE: Glory to God in the highest!

Meditation

This is the first Sunday all of our Advent candles, as well as the Christ candle, have been lit. Each week we have identified a theme as the candles were lit and the meditation read. But today we celebrate worship in a unique way. It is not only Sunday; it is Christmas Day. This doesn't occur often.

Christmas on Sunday complicates our normal routine. On a typical Sunday we are up, dressed, and ready for church, with plenty of time for coffee and the Sunday paper. On a typical Christmas morning perhaps we're up early with the children, celebrating the giving and receiving of gifts, eating a special breakfast, picking up gift wrappings, and putting the ham or turkey into the oven.

Today we have rushed to do all this before church, and perhaps we are anxious to rush home and finish our dinner preparations before guests arrive. Christmas on Sunday seems like an interruption of our normal routine. Although we are here and celebrating on this special coincidence of dates, there's part of us that wishes we could have Sunday by itself and Christmas on a weekday instead.

But Christmas—the birth of Christ—*is* an interruption. Think of the shepherds calmly doing the routine job of watching their sheep on a clear night in the hills near Bethlehem. Suddenly, unannounced, right before them was an angel telling them of a birth—that of a Savior!

The shepherds interrupted their routine night of work and went to Bethlehem to confirm this. And indeed it was true: A baby had been born. Jesus interrupted their routine and still interrupts our routine to let us know of God's love, to show us a new way of life, and to challenge us to find Christ in all parts of our lives.

As this special Christmas Day Sunday continues, let us be grateful for Jesus' interruption of our lives.

Collect (Unison)

O Giver of Light, we offer our thanksgiving to you for interrupting our lives so that we may know your great love made known to us in Jesus, whose birth we joyously celebrate today. Amen.

Printed in the United States
75023LV00001B/1-270